DISCARDED

That's Not Hockey!

DISCARDED

By Andrée Poulin • Art by Félix Girard

annick press
toronto + berkeley

We acknowledge the support of the Canada Council for the Arts and the Ontario Arts Council, and the participation of the Government of Canada/la participation du gouvernement du Canada for our publishing activities.

Cataloging in Publication

Poulin, Andrée, author
    That's not hockey / by Andrée Poulin ; art by Félix Girard.

Issued in print and electronic formats.
ISBN 978-1-77321-051-3 (hardcover).—ISBN 978-1-77321-052-0 (PDF).—ISBN 978-1-77321-053-7 (EPUB)

    1. Plante, Jacques, 1929-1986—Juvenile fiction. I. Girard, Félix, 1988-, illustrator II. Title. III. Title: That is not hockey.

PS8581.O837T43 2018   jC813'.54   C2018-901038-X
                                                        C2018-901039-8

Published in the U.S.A. by Annick Press (U.S.) Ltd.
Distributed in Canada by University of Toronto Press.
Distributed in the U.S.A. by Publishers Group West.

Printed in China

www.annickpress.com
www.andreepoulin.ca
www.felixgirard.com

Also available as an e-book. Please visit www.annickpress.com/ebooks.html for more details.

To my dad, who played hockey well into his 70s . . .
—A.P.

In memory of my friend, Guy Levesque, another
great creator of masks
—F.G.

Jacques loves hockey. He plays it every day.
But Jacques doesn't have a hockey puck.
So he uses a tennis ball.
Hey, that's not hockey!

But this three-year-old won't be stopped.

Jacques doesn't have a goalie stick.
So his dad makes him a stick out of a tree root.
Hey, that's not hockey!

But this five-year-old won't be stopped.

Jacques is thrilled by his first goalie pads.

His dad made them out of potato sacks and wooden slats.

Hey, that's not hockey!

But this seven-year-old won't be stopped.

At fifteen, Jacques plays goal for a factory team in Shawinigan.
He's very proud to earn fifty cents a game.

At twenty-one, his dream comes true.
He's hired as goalie for the Montreal Canadiens.
Now that's hockey!

Jacques Plante is quick and agile.
Hockey fans call him "Jake the Snake."
But he plays like no other goalie.
He leaves the crease to stop pucks.

He passes the puck to his defensemen
behind the net.
Hey, that's not hockey!

But Jacques won't be stopped.
He loves reinventing the game!

Jacques blocks thousands of pucks.
He leads his team to victory but his face suffers badly.
Broken jawbone.
Broken right cheekbone.
Broken left cheekbone.
Broken nose—four times.
Hairline fracture of the skull.
More than two hundred stitches for cuts
to his face and head!

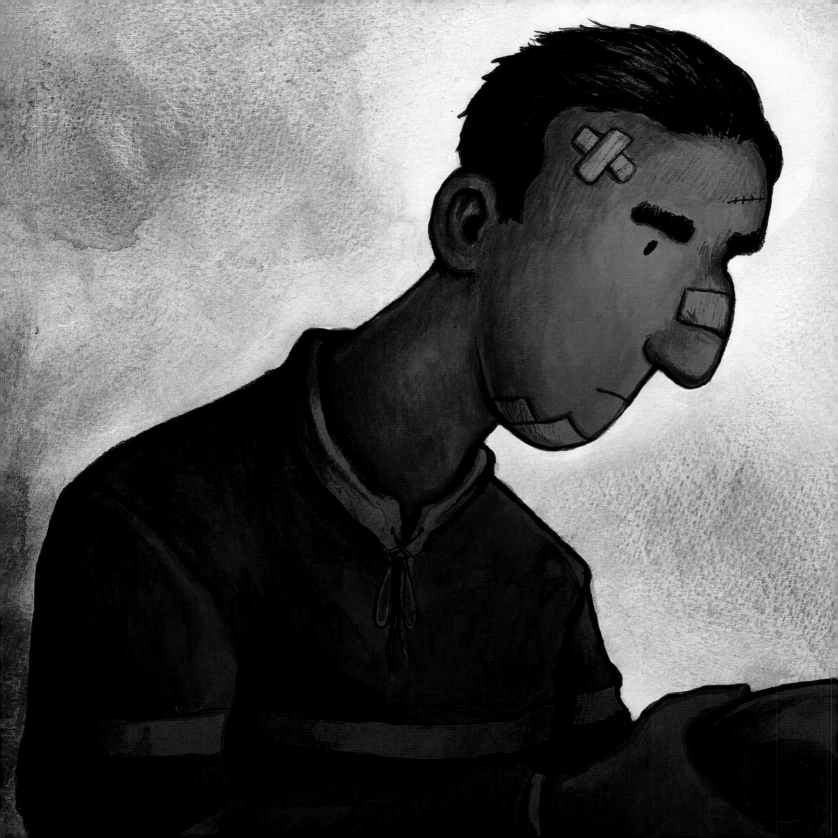

Jacques knows hockey goalies often get hurt.
He knows a slap shot to his eye could end his career.
But he never complains.
He learns to live with the fear.
And the pain.

Until one day . . .
Enough injuries! Enough pain!
Jacques doesn't want another puck in the face.
So next practice, he shows up . . .

. . . wearing a face mask.
Made of fiberglass.
A goalie mask.
Hey, that's not hockey!

The team's coach, Toe Blake, is not happy:
"This mask is too heavy!
Too hot!
You won't see the puck!
You can't wear that thing in the game!"

Then, on a cold November night in 1959, hockey changes forever.
Jacques is in net at Madison Square Garden, New York.
A Rangers player winds up and blasts a hard shot.
BANG!

Jacques is hit, square in the face.
A gash runs from his nose to his mouth.
His blood splatters the ice red.
The goalie is rushed to the dressing room.
The doctor sews up the gash.

Despite the pain, Jacques wants to finish
the game.
On one condition . . .

"I'm not playing without my mask," says Jacques.
Coach Blake is furious.
But no goalie means no game.

Jacques fits the mask over his swollen nose and mouth.
He gets back on the ice . . .

. . . with his face covered.

The other team is surprised.
And a bit scared.
Hockey fans are outraged.
The crowd boos the masked goalie.
Hey, that's not hockey!

But Jacques Plante won't be stopped.
The Canadiens beat the Rangers 4 to 1.

From then on, Jacques wears his mask at every game.
Reporters, players, goaltenders, and crowds continue to tease and taunt him:
"Hey, that's not hockey!"

But Jacques won't be bullied.
With the mask on, he feels more confident.
More daring.
But most of all, he feels . . .
safer.

A fan asks him:
"Are you scared to play without a mask?"
The goalie replies:
"If you jumped out of a plane without a
 parachute, would that make you brave?"
The Canadiens keep on winning games.

Jacques keeps wearing his mask. Little by little, hockey fans stop teasing him.

At the end of the season, the Canadiens win the Stanley Cup.
And Jacques Plante has a new nickname: The Masked Marvel.
He wore number one.
And he became number one.
Now that's hockey!

Jacques Plante, an amazing goalie!

Jacques Plante helped the Montreal Canadiens win six Stanley Cups.
He also won seven Vezina trophies for best goaltender.

He died in 1986.
In 1995, the Canadiens honored their famous goalie by retiring his jersey number forever.

Helmets and face masks are now standard equipment in hockey.
It all started with Jacques's brave defiance.
His guts and smarts changed the face of hockey **forever**.